INFERNO OF COLOR

THE BLAZING PALETTE OF AUTUMN

BY

PAUL SIMANAUSKAS

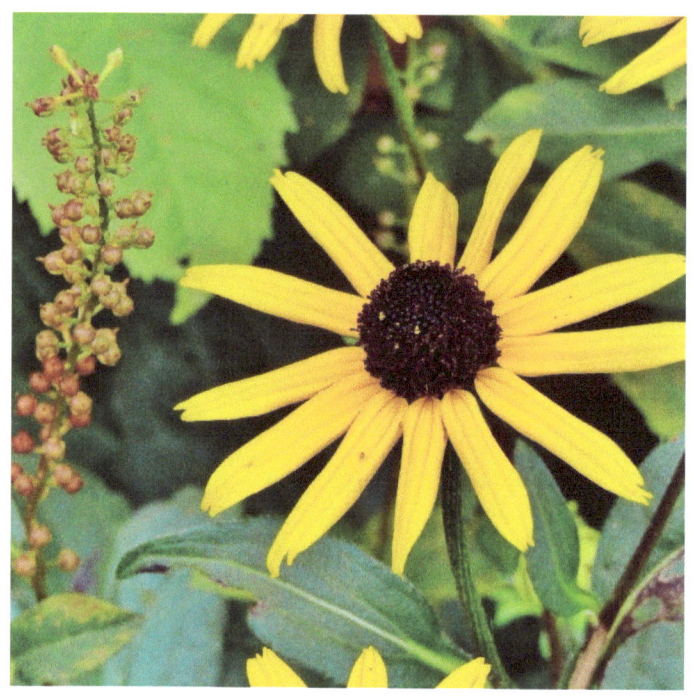

The sweet colors of summer are fleeting.
Picnics, parades, barbecues and gentle
breezes, punctuated by the occasional gusty
storm promise easy days and energetic
nights.

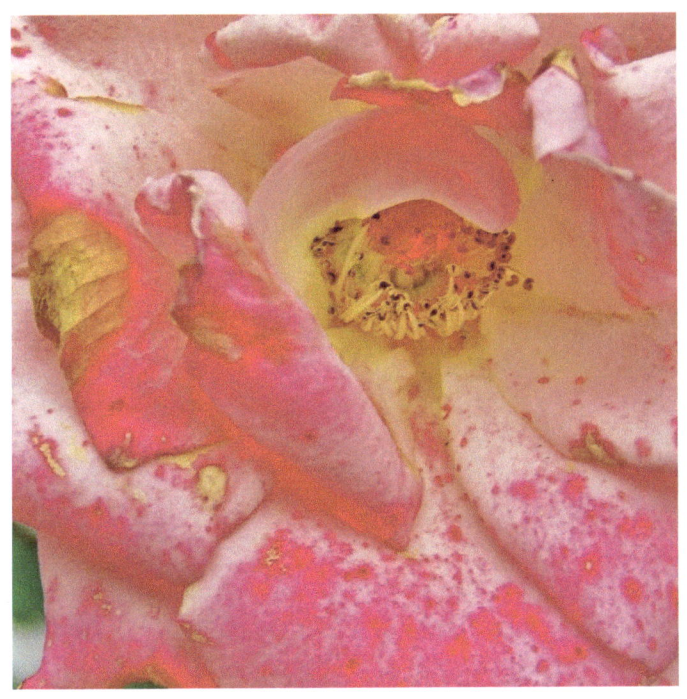

However, as summer wanes, even the brightest blooms fades. A never-ending cycle of life and death continues as the days grow short and nights become crisp.

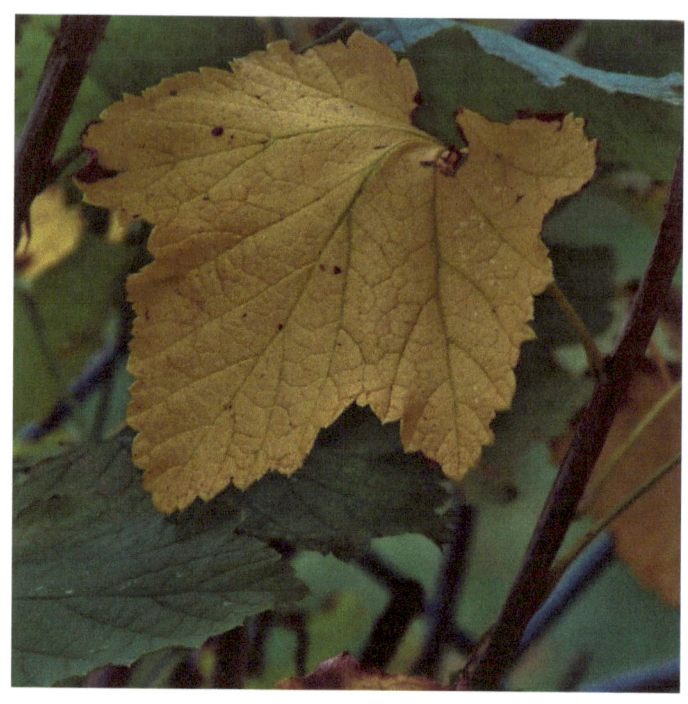

Starting slowly, the green leaves of the warmer months begin to gently relent to the coming winter chill.

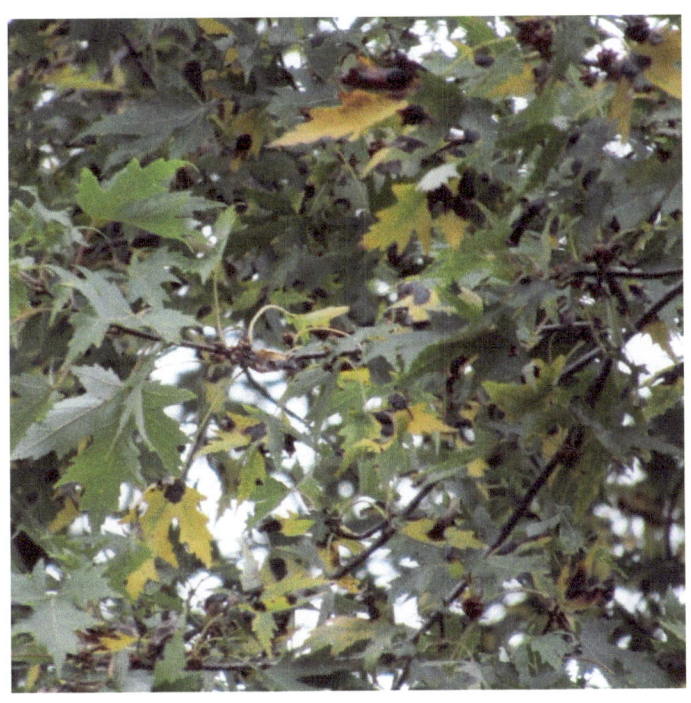

It starts with one brave leaf, unafraid of fate, beginning its metamorphosis. Soon, others will follow.

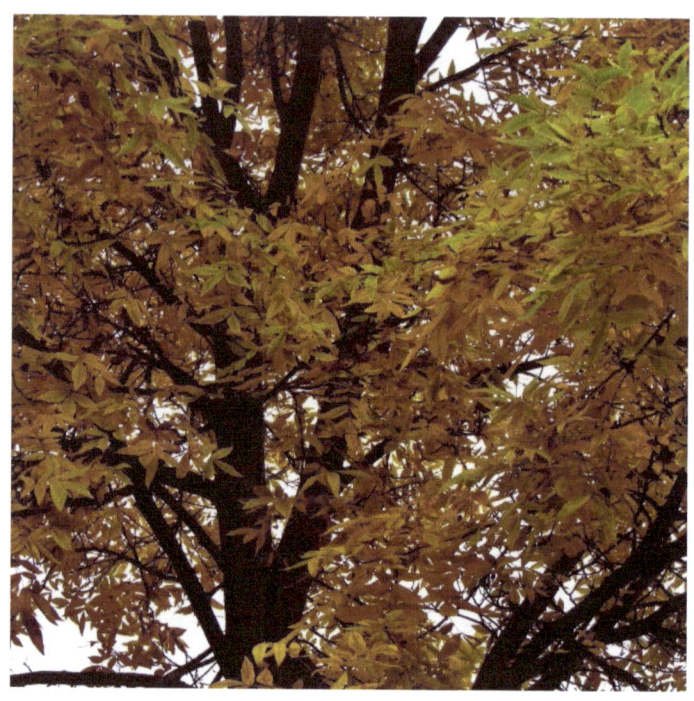

Seemingly within the blink of an eye, the world becomes gilded.

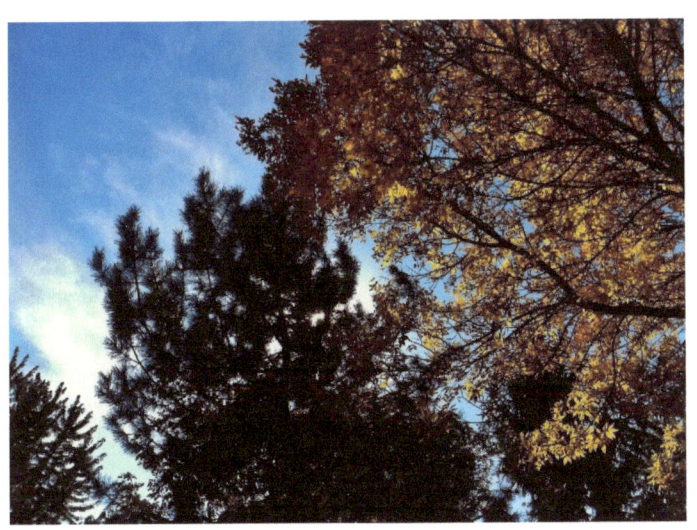

When amber kisses azure.

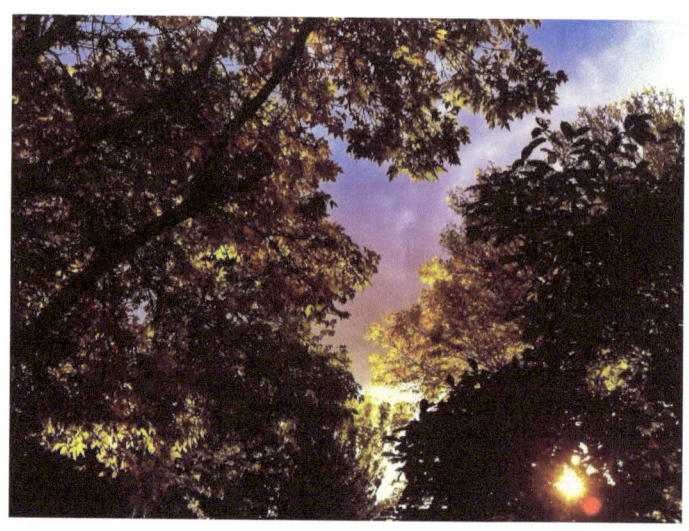

When golden sunlight peeks through golden leaves.

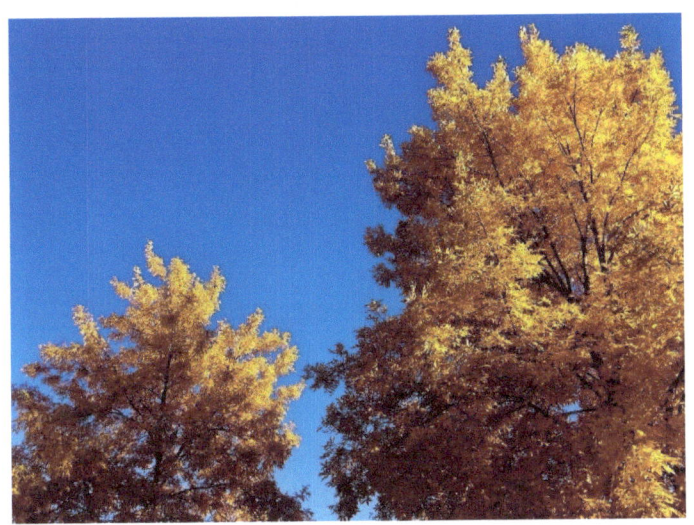

And a beacon of color lights up the world.

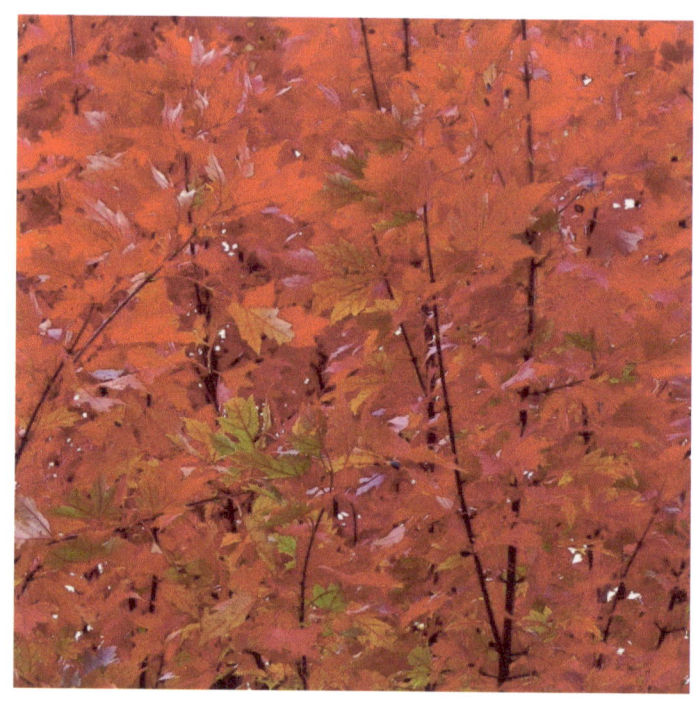

Until the trees are seemingly consumed by fire, blazing brilliantly.

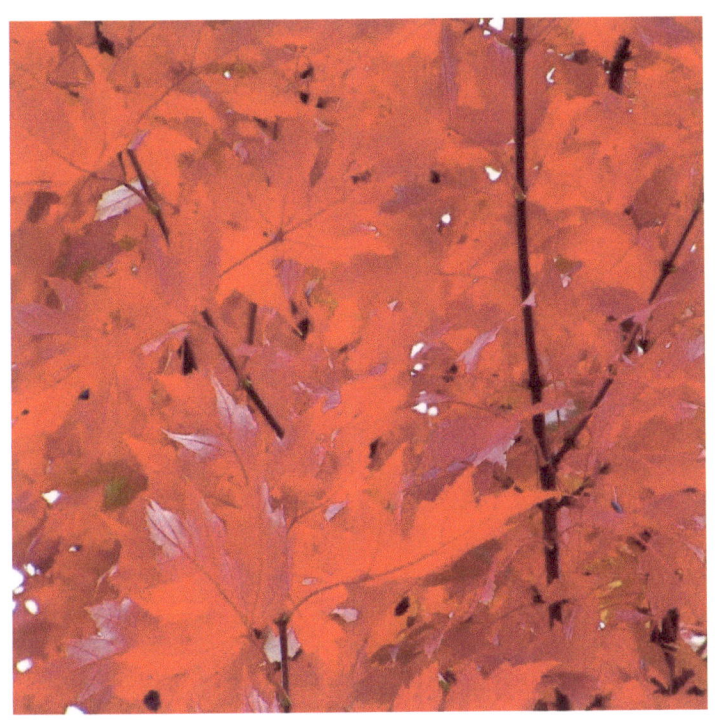

Warming our hearts before the cold, white blanket of snow envelops us in quiet forgetfulness.

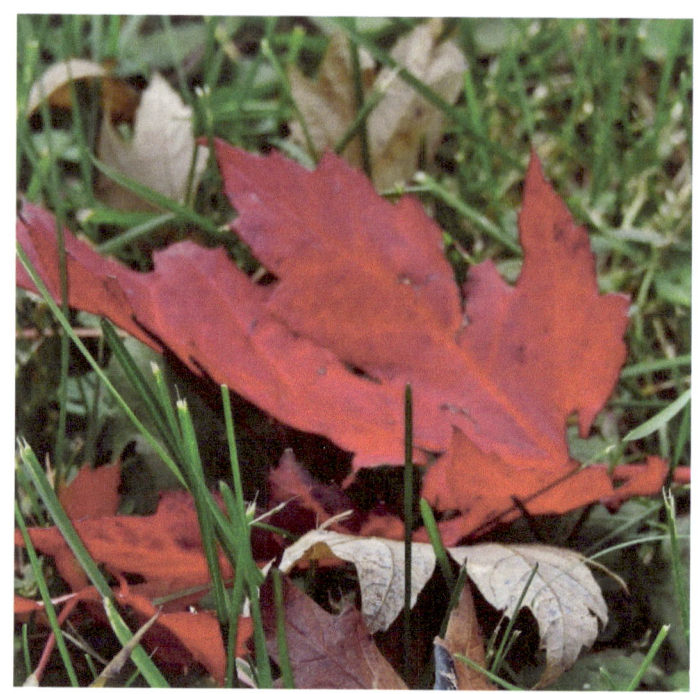

The leaves fall. One by one…

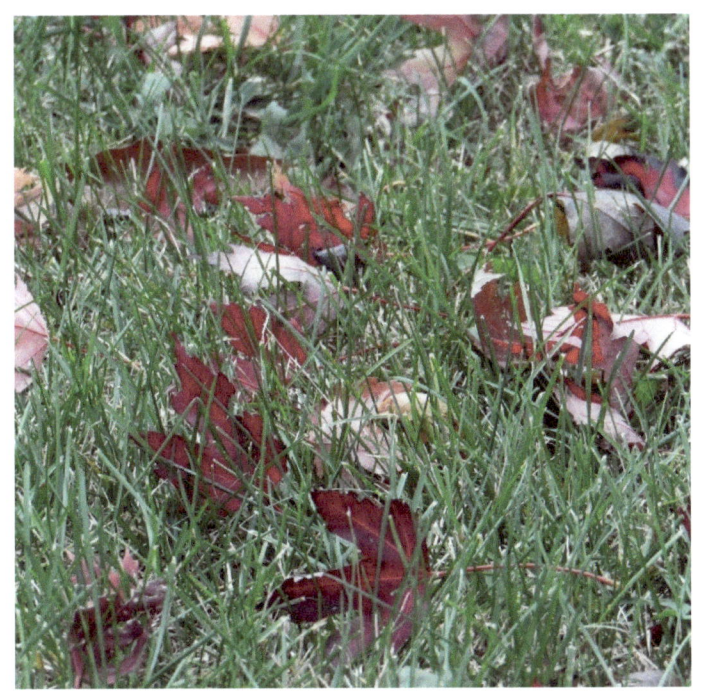

And then in droves and swarms.

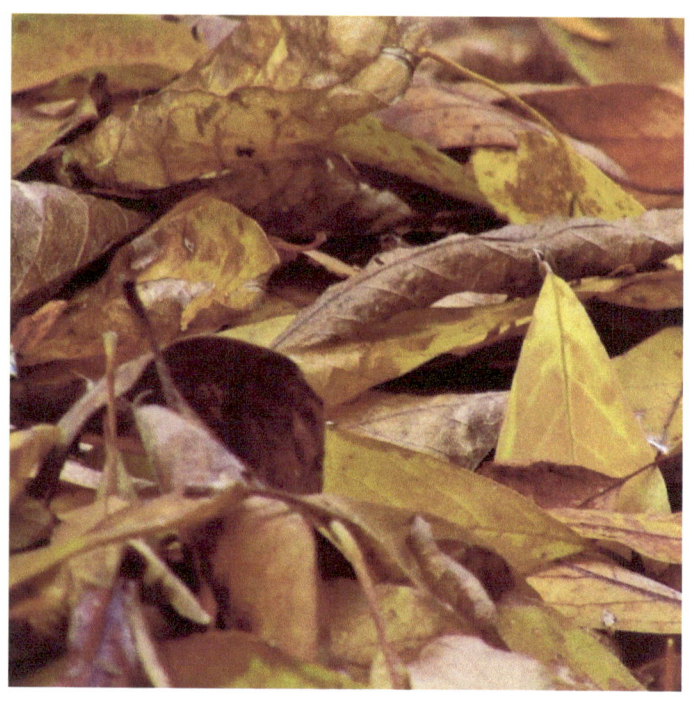

*The color fades from those leaves, decaying
slowly upon the soil which nourished it
when the days were long.*

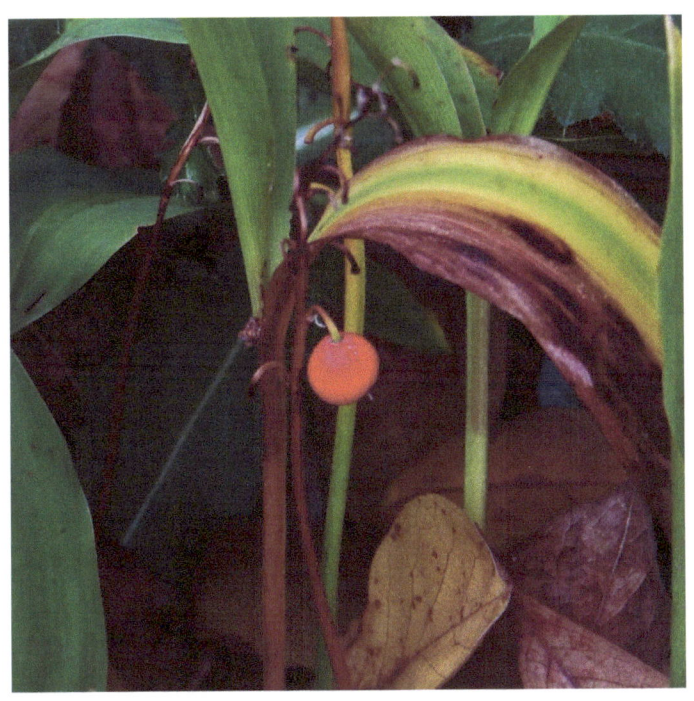

Hidden amongst the death and decay, new life waits for the frosts to melt and the sun to coax roots and buds from the dark soil.

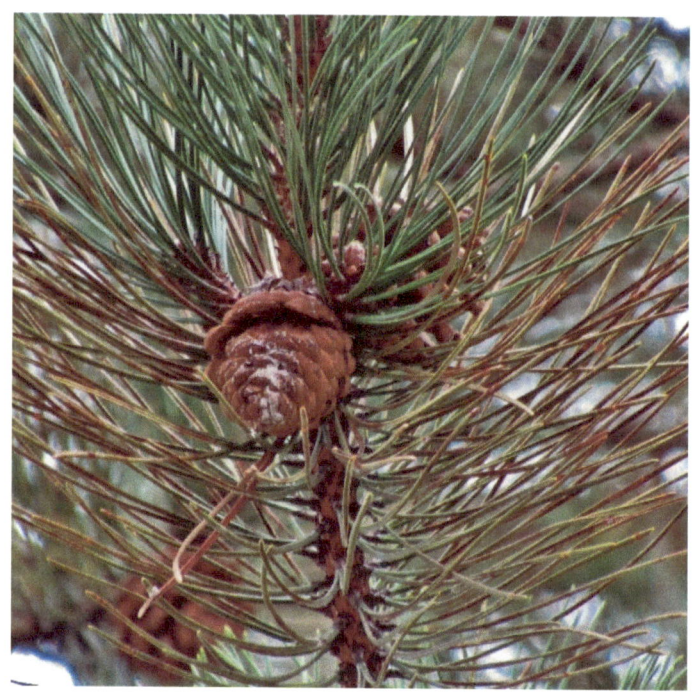

Patient, biding time, waiting for just the right time to fall and start the cycle again.

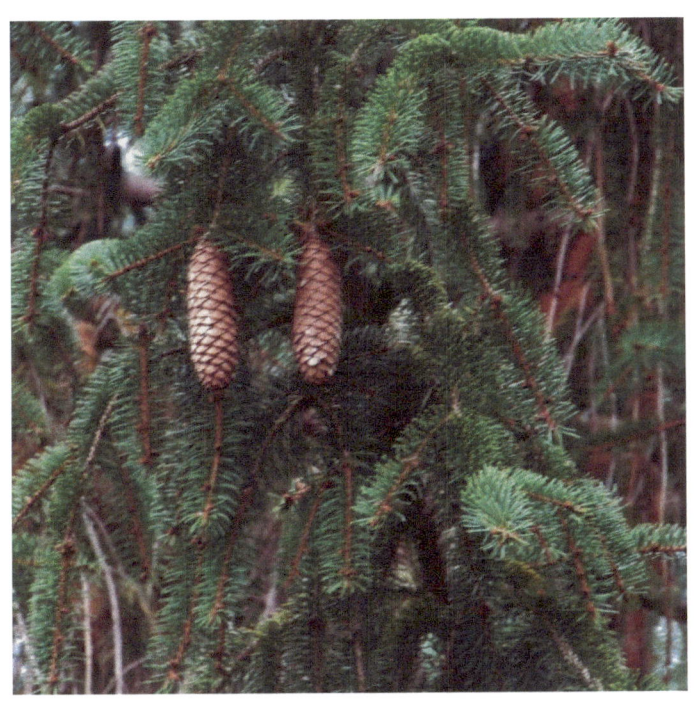

*The fruits of sun, showers, soil, and wind
grows ever larger upon the bough.*

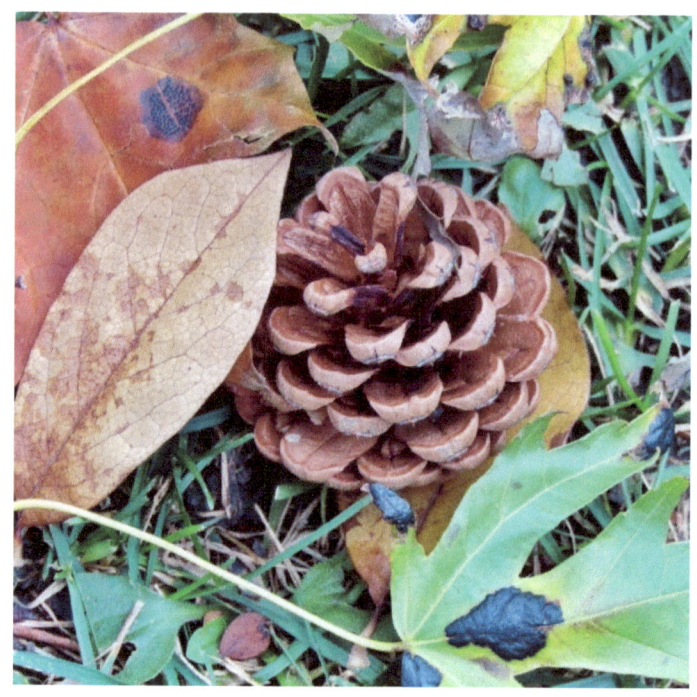

Eagerly waiting to meet the earthly cradle of life.

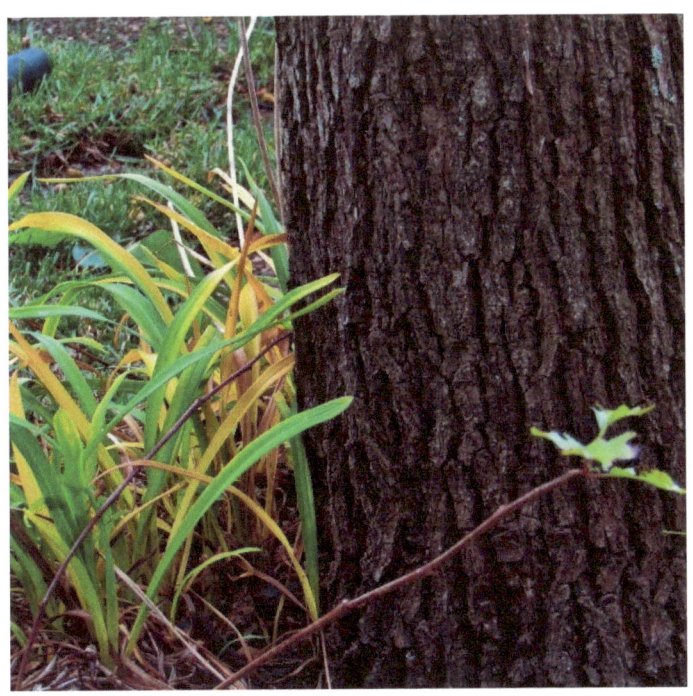

*To grow into great trees, shading us,
nourishing us, calming our souls.*

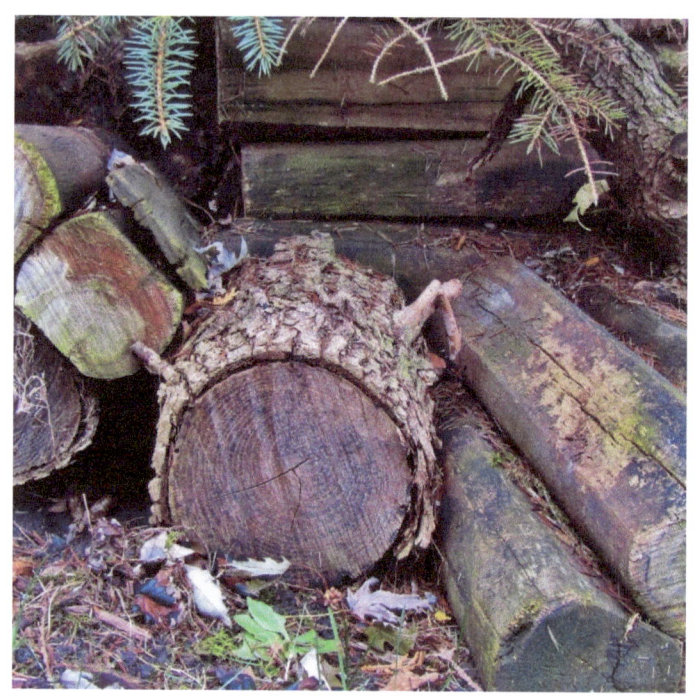

Or perhaps providing a night of merriment in front of a bonfire, or a quiet night of reflection in front of the hearth.

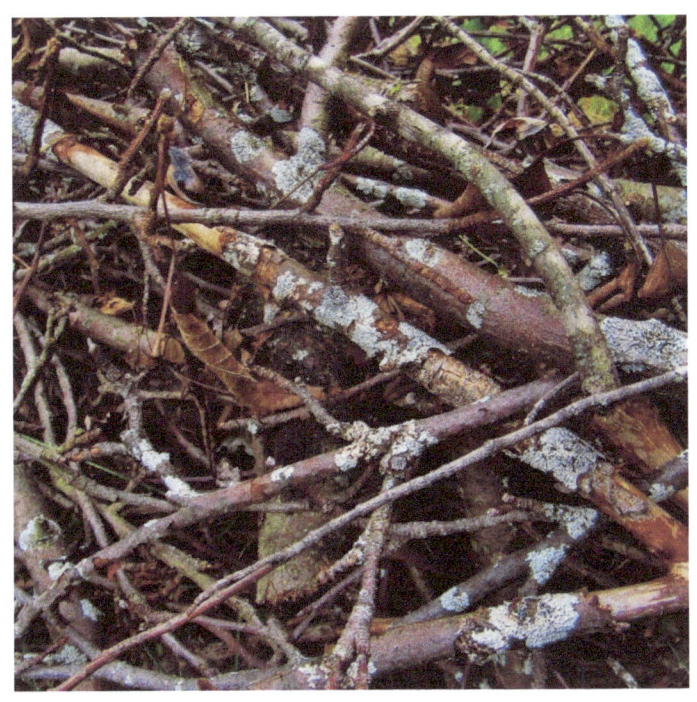

Tangling and weaving with kindling, for those crackling, blazing flames.

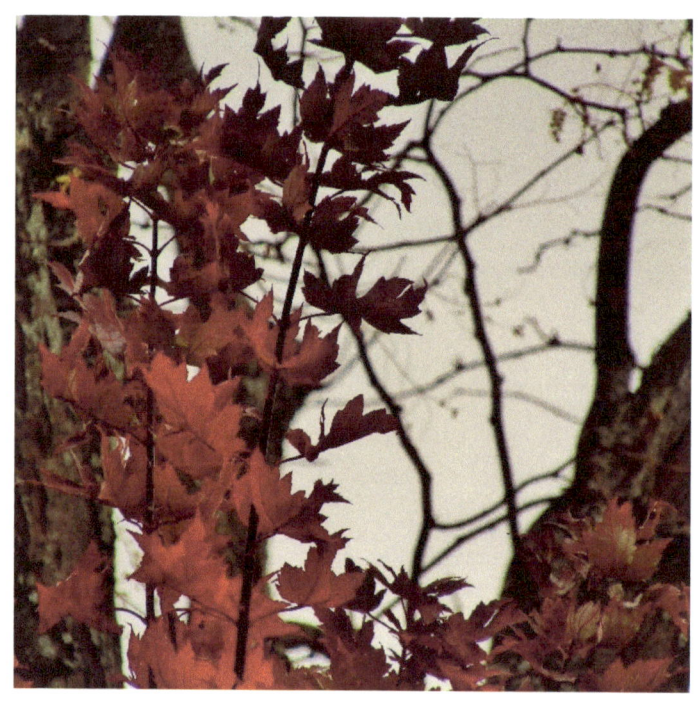

The trees seem to know this very truth,
shrouding their leaves in the hues and tones
of flame.

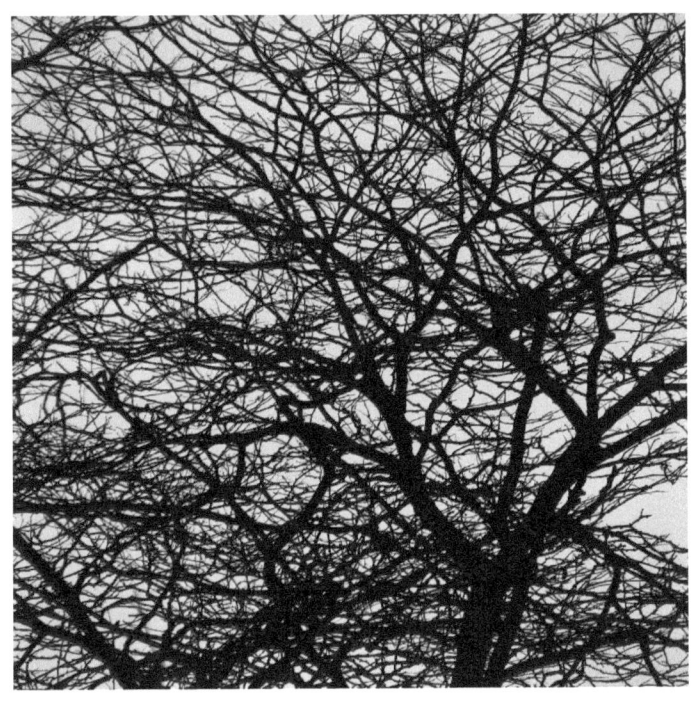

Until the great limbs are barren, biding their time until warmer days return.

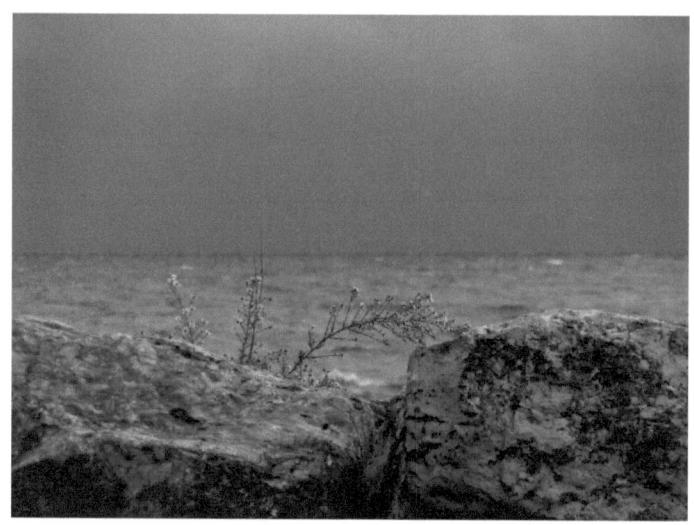

Autumn is a turbulent time.

The tempests growl and howl, like wolves
hungry for the hunt.

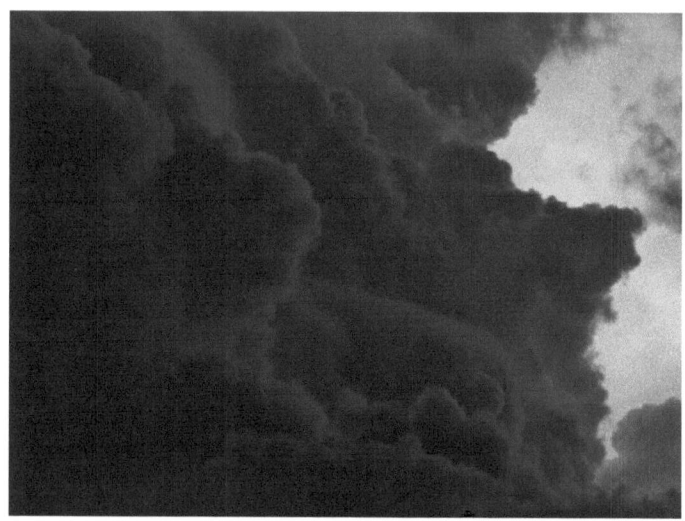

And angry clouds tower above, like
menacing titans rumbling and roaring.

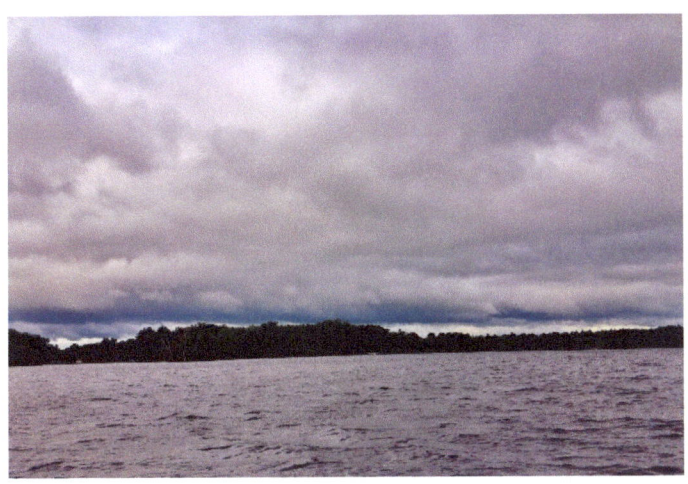

*Gathering like a dark army to cover the land
in sterile white when winter wins the battle.*

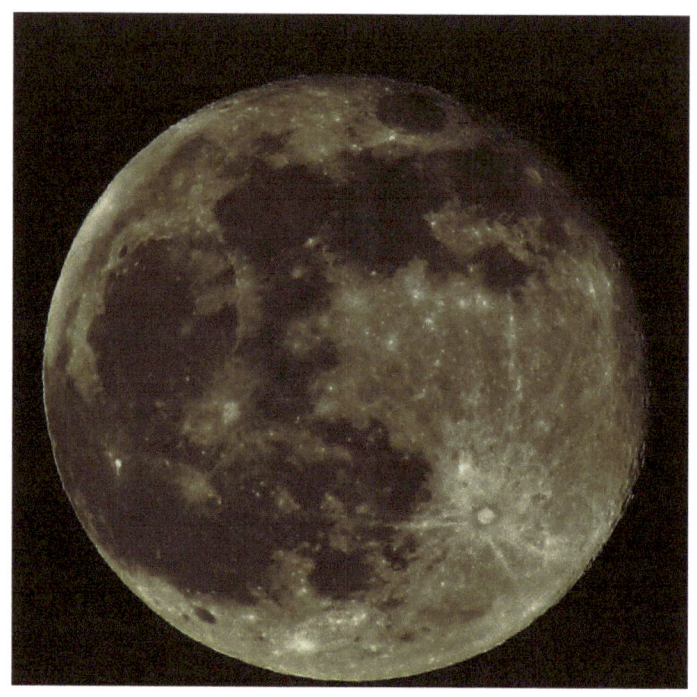

The cold moon becomes our companion as the nights grow long.

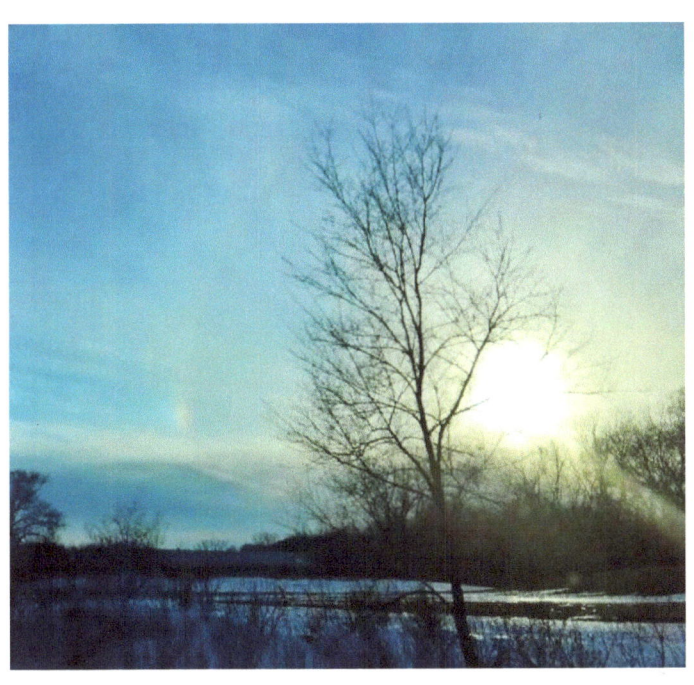

Yet, even the coldest winter promises a shining light will return.

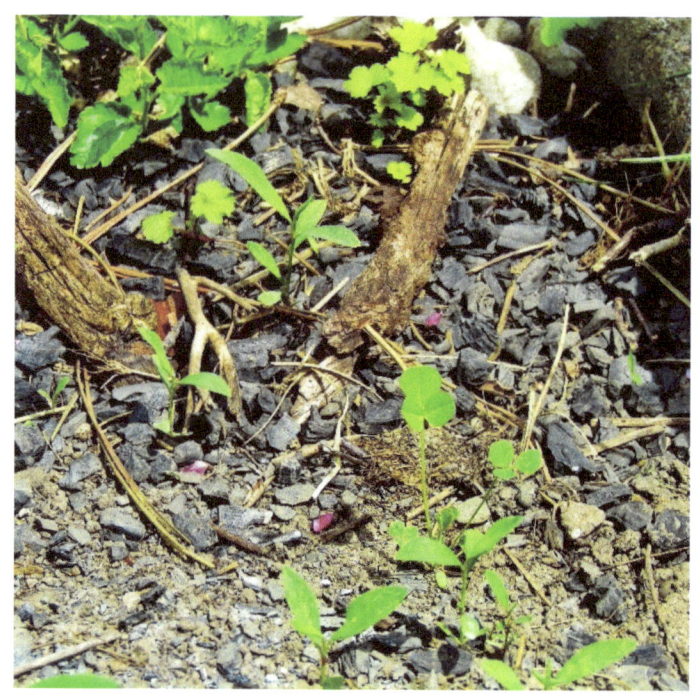

The cycle begins again, new life is born.

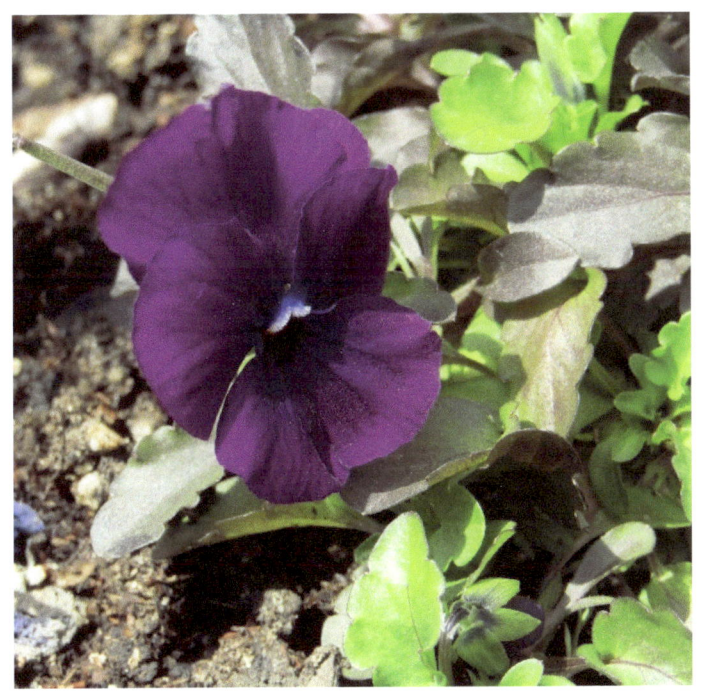

And the world is in bloom once more.

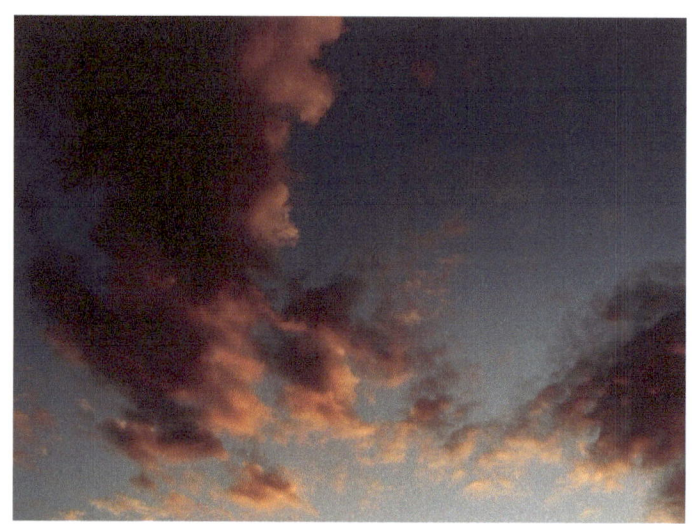

The cycle begins again.

THE FIRE BLOOM

The sweet songs of summer's day
Fades gentle to the twilight
The frosts and fogs of autumn roll
Like ghosts of a witching night

Though winter's grip is near and nigh
A gentle caress remains
Through reds and golds and amber sights
A treasure to the eye

A time of change and cleansing nears
The chilling winds remind
The seasons are all intertwined
Like hopes, dreams, and fears

A torch is lit upon the land
A beacon to guide us home
Waves crash upon the beaten sand
Whipping up the foam

The fires are lit by trees ablaze
With leaves of embers bright
Or in the hearth on frosted days
A soul-warming sight

Copyright notice

Other Titles by
Paul Simanauskas:

Shadow's Eye
The Northern Flame
Para Bellum; Prepare for War
***
A Perfect Flaw
***
The Serpent's Banner
The Serpent's Slaughter
***
Anesidora Could Not Wait
Sanguine Anguish
***
Weathering the Storm

www.ingramcontent.com/pod-product-compliance
Lightning Source LLC
Chambersburg PA
CBHW040819200526
45159CB00024B/3045